DHARMA CATS

DHARMA CATS
Copyright © 2015 Judy Taylor
All rights reserved.

ISBN: 978-0-692-61838-7

Artwork by Christine Emma
www.christineemma.com

Book Design by Frogtown Bookmaker
Frogtownbookmaker.com

DHARMA CATS

Written by Judy Taylor

Illustrated by Christine Emma

Table of Contents

Acknowledgements i
Preface iii
Introduction vii
Developing Equanimity 2
Meditative Mindfulness 5
Shadowy Presence 8
The Empty Cat 11
From Clinging to Letting Go 14
Developing Metta 16
Cultivating the Positive Through Neuroplasticity 19
Managing Aversion 22
Anger Management 25
Snippy Snipping 28
Contemplating Impermanence While Savoring the Present 31
Cat Gratitude 36
The Compassionate Cat 40
About the Author 44

Acknowledgements

This book is dedicated to all the cats I have known and loved, from the random street cats I've befriended to my live-in cat companions.

Special thanks to:

My editor, Jude Berman, for gently working with me to shape and organize the text.

My illustrator, Christine Emma (www.christineemma.com), for doing a phenomenal job of capturing the spirit of my cats and the text.

My book designer, Beth Tashery Shannon at Frogtown Bookmaker (frogtownbookmaker.com), for merging the pieces of my book together into a polished form.

Preface

Before sunrise one warm summer morning, my mother gently roused the three of us kids. We were staying the night in a modest motel in Tucson instead of one of the small cabins where we had been lodging. Well, actually, the term "small cabin" is a glamorization. These places were little more than a cement platform walled in by mosquito netting and outfitted with cots, a picnic table, and a barbeque grill. We overnighted in a series of these setups as we made our way from the Los Angeles area to San Antonio, Texas, in our silvery blue Ford Falcon.

Before leaving Tucson, Mom wanted to give us a brief drive-through tour of the University of Arizona, her alma mater. All we could see in the dark hour were deserted streets and unlit buildings. We soon departed for the open highway. Here, too, there was little sign of life, except for the occasional pair of headlights zipping past us from the opposite direction. Since we were all too sleepyheaded to do much talking, Mom snapped on the radio to paper over the silence.

Heading east, steadily crescendoing amber light began to infuse the inky sky. When the fiery sun popped its head over the horizon, we caught sight of the sparse desert stretched out to seeming infinity in all directions. The cerulean blue sky was bathed in gold and tangerine. Something about this scene instantly moved me to tears of exalted joy. I've always appreciated the beauty of a sunrise as it dispels the calm darkness, but this experience was transcendently blissful. Being immersed in this bright, serene, and limitless landscape touched some innate resonance in me about how heaven might feel.

By the time I reached adulthood, the memory of that mystical moment impelled me to seek more of that feeling. The child of an atheist father and lapsed Catholic mother, I had no spiritual tradition to contain that yearning. I gravitated to New Age thought because it seemed to exude the mysticism I craved.

I scoured the spiritual section of my local bookstore and read voraciously. Many of the paperbacks were filled with fascination for the paranormal, yet in the mix were some Buddhist texts. Buddhism intrigued me because it seemed to match the way I naturally thought. I took the next logical step and signed up for a meditation class.

I soon drifted away from Buddhist thought due to a fundamental misunderstanding. My initial impression was that Buddhism was a pretty dour philosophy. I became stuck on the First Noble Truth, which made me think Buddhism was all about dukkha, suffering. I missed the fact that the Fourth Noble Truth offers a path out of our dukkha. And since I hadn't yet been introduced to any heart-based meditations—such as exercises to cultivate the four brahmaviharas (equanimity, loving-kindness, sympathetic joy, and compassion)—I wasn't aware that Buddhism also included some very uplifting practices.

Stuck in my misperceptions, I went back to New Age thought because it met my desire for a mystical connection and it seemed like a more upbeat path. I spent many years chasing after each new gadget, crystal, book, meditation method, and reformulated ancient technique that promised a more transcendent state. Each time, I was convinced my latest purchase would lift me into permanent nirvana. When that didn't happen, I would reflexively grasp after yet another spiritual tool. I was sure the ticket to transcendence was wrapped in the next shiny, colorful package or glib, electrifying lecture.

Then about a dozen years ago, I began to read some books by the Dalai Lama and Thich Nhat Hahn. Their heart-centered ethics and simple messages were very inspiring to me. The more I read about how craving was the cause of suffering, the more I realized that rather than leading me to happiness, New Age philosophy was stoking the flames of my dukkha. The central New Age message that tells us we can have anything we want seems to impel us to keep grasping for more.

What also troubled me about the New Age movement was the prevalent belief in and reliance upon unseen forces to guide one's life. I felt a real need for something less woo-woo and more substantial. So, with great relief, I turned to Theravada Buddhism, which felt very grounding to me.

Since then, I've been entirely ensconced in Buddhist thought. I discovered that I don't need expensive crystals, elaborate techniques, or supplications to invisible beings to attain inner peace and happiness. Simply meditating, watching my mind, being present, and letting go of craving has given me more sustained bliss than being on the constant search for another spiritual high.

The idea for this book occurred to me when I became aware that my Buddhist practice converged with my life of cat companionship. I noticed that I was naturally using my furry friends as fixtures in my meditation and mindfulness practices. Writing became a way to crystallize and share my discoveries about cats as they relate to Buddhist principles.

So, curl up in a comfortable place and enjoy Dharma Cats. And if you are fortunate enough to live with a purring feline, then hopefully she will sit with you as you read and enable you to catalyze your own insights!

Introduction

I have always been irresistibly drawn to cats. Their eyes exude a charming innocence and vulnerability that compels me to touch them. Their capricious nature is also quite amusing. In an impish mood, they might suddenly leap out at you from behind a corner. Alternately, you might find them lying in a purring puddle, completely content with the world. Then at the first hint of danger, they puff themselves up with menacing hisses and swat with their killer claws.

    I grew up in a house of cats. When I was four-years-old, the first cat to nuzzle its way into our lives was an emerald-eyed grey and white kitten. She kept showing up at our back door, with the clear intention of becoming part of the family. My sister and I couldn't stop petting her soft, cottony fur. My brother, being six, decided to name her Skippy after the peanut butter.

    Several years after Skippy adopted us, my sister and I hungered for more cats. We craved their essence as if it were candy. So, with the $5 our grandparents had given each of us for our birthdays, we bought two calico sisters. Soon after this, the fur literally began to fly as our unfixed felines begat kittens. The darting, leaping little fur balls were everywhere, mewing for mama cat and kibble.

Poor Skippy was marginalized as we turned our full attention to the newborns. She expressed her displeasure at their presence by grumbling into her food bowl everyday. Any kitten foolhardy enough to think Skippy would share her meal was instantly swiped at. Skippy would speedily inhale her chow, then skitter off to spend to rest of her day outside, far, far away from all the young upstarts.

Once the little ones had been weaned, we gave them away to eager families. Our empty-nester moms disappeared after being freed of their nurturing duties. This restored Skippy to her former reign as sole feline of the manor.

After Queen Skippy died and I went to college, I was bereft of these sweet creatures for the first time since I was young. Though I missed living with cats, I was much too busy to think of bringing a feline presence back into my life.

Then, a few years later, on a frigid December day, my boyfriend met an emaciated grey tabby at the top of Nob Hill in San Francisco. Being a compassionate soul, he couldn't turn his back on her plaintive cries for food and companionship. So he brought her to our apartment.

I decided to name her Snappy because she was a temperamental cat who might purr in your face one moment and strike out at you the next. Yet Snappy became my devoted friend. She slept atop my head at night and regarded me lovingly during the day.

A year or two later, the same boyfriend swooped up a wide-eyed calico fluff ball who had taken up residence at the auto shop across the street. This hungry, oil-streaked little thing was christened Ginger for her tawny fur. Her pelt was like cotton candy, and I became addicted to caressing and absorbing its sweetness. Ginger had an angelic aura and seemed almost too delicate for this world. But despite her fragile, otherworldly demeanor, Ginger never let Snappy intimidate her. She held her own in their daily paw fights.

When these two eventually succumbed to old age and death, I searched for another furry best friend. I soon found Tawy, a solid grey long hair. Still with me today, Tawy is a mercurial character, as many cats are. She swings from being a recluse to behaving almost dog-like in her attempts to be beside me. Tawy was my first lap cat. She'll lie in my lap for long spells while being stroked. Then she'll thank me with loud purrs and molten eyes.

Not only have these enchanting creatures been wonderful companions for me over the years, but they have also served as my teachers. After I began studying Buddhism, I started to see how naturally Buddhist these little beings are. They appear to innately possess qualities that we're encouraged to develop, such as equanimity, patience, and the ability to be fully present in the moment. Living with cats has also given me lots of opportunities to use them as objects of my dharma practice. Life with cats has never been dull.

Developing Equanimity

A cat's behavior can be maddening sometimes. One morning, Tawy was sitting in front of our sliding glass door. She was staring at it with such intensity that it seemed as if she were trying to command the door to open with the power of her mind. To help her along, I interrupted my work to push the door ajar. But instead of bounding out, Tawy continued to squat there.

"You want out?" I prompted, with a slight edge to my voice.

She remained stationary, like a stone Buddha.

"Don't you want out, Tawy?" I added with a bit more irritation. Then, slamming the door shut, I shouted, "So why are you sitting there like you want out, you damn cat?"

Wide-eyed, Tawy peered up at me as if to implore, "And why are you yelling at me?"

Yes indeed, why was I shouting at my sweet little cat? That look of innocence reminded me that cats don't think or behave the way we do. Tawy was simply acting like the typical cat who is animated by inner meowing voices we can't fully comprehend. Isn't inscrutability part of a feline's charm? So why would I want Tawy to be more predictable?

These thoughts began to soothe my snarly mind, enabling me to notice what my impatience was doing to me. My agitation had tightened my shoulder muscles and produced an acid taste in my mouth. These damaging effects told me that I needed to be more accepting of crazy cat behavior or suffer the physical consequences.

Now if Tawy suddenly starts racing around the house for no apparent reason, stares at me intensely, or sits in front of doors without wanting to go out, I know a little mindfulness will help me take such confounding behavior in stride. A little dose of equanimity softens my cat-titude.

Meditative Mindfulness

Ever try sleeping during a noisy party or within earshot of a blaring stereo? Impossible, right? Well, somehow all the cats I've known seem to be able to doze off in such chaotic environments. I am constantly amazed at how blissfully tuned out they appear to be in the midst of such cacophony. Nothing seems to prevent these little lions from getting their beauty rest.

Yet, at the same time, they seem keenly attuned to their exterior environment. While appearing to be sleeping peacefully, their little ears flicker and move occasionally to follow sounds. Usually, however, they do not allow such noises to distract them from their main occupation in life. Instead, they hunker down more deeply into the sleep mode.

Observing them, I realize that they are masters of mindfulness. I try to call to mind their behavior sometimes during meditation. Mimicking the cat, I become aware of all the sounds in the room, but don't react to any of them nor open my eyes to determine their source. My skin may scream out for me to scratch it or tantalizing thoughts may dance across my mind. Instead of following these intrusive sensations, I remind myself to remain steadfastly mindful. I gently guide my mind back to the breath. In this way, I work to acquire a quality of mindfulness that seems innate to the cat.

Shadowy Presence

I admire cats for their ability to be fully present. They seem completely absorbed in whatever they're doing, whether it's napping, observing creepy crawlies in the dirt, or chomping down their food. Not only do they seem utterly present in the moment, but they also appear to be quite content within it. Their peaceful demeanor makes me doubt that their minds are elsewhere. They're not thinking up a better mouse-catching strategy or worrying about how they destroyed the sofa.

When I first brought Tawy home from the animal shelter, I almost named her Shadow for her charcoal grey fur and tendency to loiter closely behind me. Now she hovers near me because she either wants to be fed or craves my companionship. While I enjoy her company, her shadowing habit can be annoyingly dangerous. It's too easy for me to accidentally step on her paws or tail. And when I do so, I feel horrible. I apologize by rubbing the hurt spot and speaking to her in loving tones.

Yet, quite quickly after such incidents, Tawy will be back behind me like the shadow I can't shake. I gather that since she is so much in the present moment, she's not dwelling on the past (the accident) nor is she thinking about the future (that the same

behavior might put her in jeopardy of being squashed again). Tawy is only focused on the now.

Tawy always seems to have complete trust in my ability to keep her safe. Though I find her faith in me quite charming, I know I must live up to her confidence. This means I need to be more mindful of her whereabouts as I move around the house.

Now instead of seeing Tawy's shadowing behavior as an inconvenience, I view it as an aid to mindfulness. I'm thankful that her actions are forcing me to develop the very quality of awareness I so admire in her!

The Empty Cat

When I look at a cat, she meets my gaze with frankness and a solid presence of being. There is no artifice, no attempt to project a more flattering picture of herself to others. It's hard to imagine that cats spend any time whatsoever in constructing and maintaining a self-image. I doubt they even have a concept of selfness. They just react to the outside world instinctively, without an apparent need to form identities.

This way of being is in contrast with how we are as humans. We tend to think of ourselves in terms of our identities. We see ourselves in relationship to others (brother, coworker, friend); in accordance with our views and opinions (Democrat, conservative, open-minded); based upon our economic status or occupation (middle-class, engineer, construction worker); in line with our affiliations, whether national, religious, or cultural (Japanese, Catholic, indigenous); or according to our personal characteristics (shy, cheerful, Type A). We commonly consider these aspects of ourselves as fixed, constant, and intrinsic.

Yet, when I call to mind how I was in childhood or even a year ago, it's easy to see how I've grown and changed. I know I'm not the tireless little girl I once was, and my interest in Buddhism tells me I am not the same as I used to be. This points to the lack of a permanent self.

The idea of not having a fixed inner core can be quite unsettling and scary. Yet, cats don't appear to be tortured by such thoughts. Why can't I try to be more like cats in this regard? This might ease my queasiness over my lack of a solid self.

So when I want to examine and work at releasing my sense of selfness, I just observe Tawy. Seeing her curled up on the couch napping peacefully, I watch as her quiet breath gently sways her midsection. If she happens to look up at me, her gaze is so naked and unassuming. It's doubtful she's worrying about what I think of her. There is no hint of an ulterior motive or ruse.

I notice that Tawy shifts in and out of modes of being. She is the ultimate empty cat—empty of a permanent self. When Tawy feels fear, it is very apparent in her wide-eyed look and hissing. When she's experiencing love, it is demonstrated directly through her soft eyes, nuzzling gestures, and purrs.

Tawy was an energetic youngster when she arrived at my home 11 years ago. Now, at 14, her hearing isn't as keen and she has trouble jumping onto my lap due to an arthritic hip.

As I contemplate these facets of Tawy, I can plainly see that I am subject to the same forces of impermanence in body and in mind. These revelations immediately serve to loosen my grip on selfness. I know I am just as empty of a permanent self as Tawy is.

From Clinging to Letting Go

I love to snuggle and sleep with my cats. Listening to their rhythmic purring, feeling their cozy softness, and watching their happy paws knead the blankets are so comforting to me. Yet, they rarely linger with me for as long as I want. Tawy's prone to getting settled, and then without warning, she will bound out of my embrace and off the bed. I am left clinging to the rapidly fading imprint of her warmth and sweetness.

Instead of wallowing in my cravings for Tawy's companionship, I realized that I can use her departures as opportunities to observe my clinging tendencies. When I do that, I see that my unwholesome desires are like icky, sticky claws grasping at her fur. I seem to be trying to cage the untamable.

To help me release these feelings, I reflect on a few possible reasons for Tawy's sudden flight off the bed. Perhaps she got too warm under the covers. Or maybe she heard a noise she wanted to investigate. Or perhaps she needed to appease the god of hunger. Who knows? I just know that regarding such possibilities begins to temper my ever-desiring soul.

Developing Metta

Years ago, I was in a class where we were asked to generate feelings of love. Normally, it's difficult to spontaneously drum up such emotions. But the teacher suggested that we start by thinking of someone we loved or felt warmly about. I mentally scrolled through images of my favorite friends and family members, but quickly realized that the level of my feelings for each fluctuated over time. If things were going well between us, I would be favorably inclined toward them. But if we'd recently had a disagreement, it was a lot harder for me to feel good about them. Yet when I thought of any of my cats, I automatically felt love for them—no matter how many times Snappy unreeled the toilet paper all over the floor or Tawy pooped on the carpet.

So, since then, visualizing one of my cats in the first category of metta practice has been a great way for me to instantly kindle feelings of loving-kindness. Cats are like the match that sparks my metta. Once this flame has been lit, I have a cauldron of positive feelings to draw upon when doing my metta exercises, which involve directing love toward different types of individuals. I find that when my heart has been warmed up in this way, it's much

easier to send kindly feelings toward myself and then extend them toward someone in the "neutral person category" and even toward someone in the "difficult person" category.

I begin by picturing one of my cats. For instance, I visualize Tawy lying in front of me. I see her tenderhearted green eyes and her silken, smoky-colored fur. Then I get a sense of her gentle demeanor. Just imagining her like this in my mind's eye easily evokes affectionate feelings. These positive emotions are so strong that I generally have no problem sustaining them throughout the remaining stages of my metta practice. If the loving-kindness starts to ebb away, I refresh my picture of Tawy and the sunny emotions come roaring right back to life like a fire that's been reignited.

Cultivating the Positive Through Neuroplasticity

According to Rick Hanson, author of *Buddha's Brain*, the natural tendency of our mind is to focus on the negative. This is a holdover from our ancestry, when we had to be constantly on the alert for any potential threat. This skew of mind kept us alive then, but left us with a brain that tends to notice more of what's wrong rather than what's right.

Hanson suggests that if we'd like to shift this proclivity, we can use wise effort to cultivate more positive states of mind. The concept of neuroplasticity can help us here. Neuroplasticity means that our brains are capable of developing fresh pathways as we learn new behaviors and alter our mindset. We can definitely rewire our brain's neural structure for the better.

I've applied these teachings in many areas of my life. One of these is simply enjoying my cat's company. For instance, I start by being completely mindful of the pure pleasure I experience while being with Tawy. Then I might bring my awareness to her comforting warmth. Or I take tactile pleasure in the softness of her fur. And since she's usually purring, I pay attention to that deeply soothing hum.

Rick Hanson says that we must savor these positive sensations and emotions for as long as we can—at least five to twenty seconds—for new neural connections to form in the brain. So, I reflect on these tangible aspects while I let the impressions sink into my being. It helps to imagine bathing in these sensations, like sitting in a warm tub filled with healing mineral waters. The idea is not to cling to the impressions, but rather to soak in them so they can rework the brain in a more wholesome direction.

Managing Aversion

Cohabitating with cats has brought me face-to-face with my aversive nature. An especially rich place for me to observe it has been around cat poop. Like most people, I am disgusted by the wretched smell of deposits in the litter box. Another thing I find distasteful is discovering a piece of poop stuck to my cat's back fur. This not only makes them a stinky mess, but also makes cleaning them quite trying. During the cleanup, my cats will fuss and whine like cranky babies getting their diapers changed.

    I used to routinely express my aversion by either grumbling about the mess to be cleaned up or by complaining about the putrid smell. I assumed the best way to deal with emotions was to vent them outwardly, like letting steam escape from a pressure cooker. Popular therapies advised us to grab a pillow, scream into it, and pound it with all our might. This was believed to be the healthy way to process emotions.

    After I began learning about neuroplasticity, I understood that the mechanisms of the brain can work for us or against us. By venting and indulging our unwholesome emotions, we unwittingly reinforce our negative patterns of reactivity and make it much more likely that our uncomfortable feelings will resurface

repeatedly. As we allow these emotions to run amok in our minds and give rise to unwise actions, they etch deeper and deeper grooves in our brains. These ingrained patterns then become very entrenched, and dedicated work is required to extinguish them.

With this knowledge in mind, I decided to become more mindful of what was going on inside me. The first thing I noticed was that the smell of excrement produced a familiar sense of repulsion in me. Then upon seeing the litter strewn across the floor, I became aware of how warm my body was and how my muscles had started to contract in irritation. Following close on the heels of these sensations was my impulse to vent all my uncomfortable feelings. Instead of doing so, I continued to observe my intense emotions and refrained from stoking the fire of my emotions with stories about how annoying it was to have to take care of the smelly mess.

I like to remind myself that part of cat cohabitation involves some labor and repugnant experiences. I know that the pleasure of their purry, furry companionship far outweighs the inconvenience of cleaning up after them. Remembering to be thankful for the fact that despite all my other allergies, I am not allergic to cat dander helps me shift my cat-titude toward gratitude.

I am happy to report that these mindfulness practices have substantially tamed my emotions. I have brought in more awareness when dealing with cat crap. Over time, I have seen that although my irritable and disgusted feelings may still arise, they have lost some of their force and heat. They mumble to me now, without kidnapping me and making me a prisoner of my aversive nature.

Anger Management

Because our animal companion's reactions are so genuine, they can provide us with valuable feedback. Once while cooking, I became infuriated with a burner that had stopped working properly. Being already stressed and not feeling well, I was disinclined to skillfully handle my anger. I only wanted to adamantly and outwardly express my frustration in that moment. So I pounded my fist on the counter and yelled at the walls.

Suddenly I remembered I was not alone. Last time I checked, Ginger and Snappy were lounging behind me in the kitchen. Wondering if they were still there, I spun around to find them both wide-eyed and frozen in place. The shocked, scared looks on their faces jolted me back to sanity and caused me to start laughing. How ridiculous of me to frighten the cats with my stupid temper tantrum! I needed to provide them with a quiet, safe environment because they had finely attuned hearing and a heightened awareness of danger. Fortunately, my laughter immediately softened their alarmed looks.

As soon as my amusement faded, my cheeks grew hot with embarrassment. I wondered if the neighbors heard me through the walls. This uncomfortable thought increased my willingness to handle my rising ire with greater wisdom.

Since then, the searing memory of my cats' startled faces has prompted me to put some mindfulness between my heated feelings and my actions. This in-the-moment awareness has been the key to curtailing some of my knee-jerk reactions made in anger.

Snippy Snipping

If you've ever tried to trim a cat's nails, you know that it can be a potentially dangerous and nerve-wracking experience. Great care must be taken to avoid cutting their nails too short. Since there are nerves and blood vessels in the lower part of a cat's nail, a snip too low can result in blood and a yelp of pain. Cats also don't like to be pinned down or have their claws fussed with. It's as if they're staunchly defending their right to keep their little paw daggers sharpened and ready for use.

To avoid the nail-trimming ordeal, most people opt to have a pet groomer do the deed. But with Tawy, I have bravely (or maybe I should say stupidly) decided to undertake the job myself.

When I first started cutting her nails, Tawy would fidget as soon as I grasped her paw. I immediately got agitated and mindlessly raised my voice at her to sit still. This of course, made things much worse. Tawy squirmed even more and tried to leap out of my grasp. I felt increasingly anxious about keeping her pinned down so I could finish the job. More yelling and struggling ensued.

Fortunately, I quickly realized that my nervous reactions were counterproductive. I decided to be more mindful of how I conduct

myself throughout the nail-cutting routine. I needed to be more aware of my emotions and not let them rule my behavior.

Instead of my heavy-handed approach, I now begin by speaking to Tawy in a soft, calm, and soothing manner, belying any inner tension. I then pick her up, sit down on the carpet, and place her firmly between my legs. Next, I try to make her as comfortable as possible by petting and brushing her soft fur. If she starts purring, I know I've succeeded in calming her. I massage her paws a bit before proceeding to subtly and swiftly snip her claws.

Not only can I now accomplish this task without Tawy's resistance, but also I can get the job done in short order. With a few quick clips, I can blunt her little daggers so they can't do any serious damage. The side benefit is that my increased awareness calms me, too!

Contemplating Impermanence While Savoring the Present

During late February I usually grow quite weary of the unending stream of frigid, sunless days. At that point, it seems as if winter will continue interminably. But when I remind myself that it won't be this dreary forever, I can better tolerate the unwelcome weather. I reflect on the fact that spring will come. Warming rays will break through the fog and thaw the stone cold earth. In this way, contemplating the inevitable process of change positively shifts my feelings about the present.

Nothing makes this transition more vivid to me than looking out at my jasmine vines. Seeing the freshly emerging pink buds gives me a jolt of pleasant anticipation. They tell me that spring will soon be here. I eagerly await the unfolding of these shoots so that they can emit their sweet, intoxicating perfume. Once they do, it's like candy for my sense of smell! I stick my nose into the bouquets and inhale deeply of their heavenly aroma. Then at night, when their scent is the strongest, I fling open the back door and savor a good, long drag of the jasmine-filled air until the chill forces me back indoors.

Yet, I am highly aware that this bounty has a short bloom season, so I remind myself to enjoy every last sniff to the fullest extent. Fortunately for me, these flowers fade out gradually. Their dwindling presence eases me into being without them for the rest of the year.

When Ginger was around fourteen, she started to have a few health issues. Having to take extra care of her naturally sharpened my awareness of her mortality. But I was still under the kind of delusion we tell ourselves in such circumstances: that our dear pet will live endlessly as long as any health issues are properly managed. I would trundle her off to the holistic vet every couple months for acupuncture treatments and refills of her herbal prescriptions. This routine seemed to keep her from getting worse.

Then at about sixteen and a half, Ginger suddenly began eating less. Despite my plying her with the tastiest of tidbits, her food intake dwindled to nothing. At that point, I took my withering companion to the vet.

After assessing Ginger thoroughly, she said, "I can feel she's lost her fight. Before, she always seemed willing to go along with our treatments, but now I fear she's lost her will." She paused. "I'm afraid she's dying."

My heart sank and my throat constricted. Ginger had always graced my home with a purity and innocence that brought out my softer side. I dreaded the day I could no longer peer into her gigantic luminous eyes and feel the gentle warmth of her affection.

My vet said she might last a week without eating, so I prepared to spend as much of this time with her as possible. She seemed to crave my companionship then as much as I yearned to drink up her fading essence. During the day, Ginger endeavored

to be near me wherever I was in the house. At night, she wanted to join me on the bed. But as her body weakened, I noticed that it was an increasingly herculean effort for her to leap onto the mattress. So I turned my throw pillows into stepping stones, which Ginger eagerly navigated.

I spent the next ten days watching over my declining friend. I petted her variegated patchwork coat with greater awareness, sadly noticing how her irrepressibly fluffy tufts now stuck together in gummy mats. The large green eyes I'd always enjoy looking into now held a faded aliveness, like murky pools of water. As her body fat melted away, her skin hung off her spine like drapes suspended from a curtain rod. Her backbone protruded more prominently with each passing day.

As I observed these changes in Ginger, the reality of her impending transition hung around me like a dark, damp cloak. And the unceasingly grey, chilly weather only served to deepen my gloominess.

But in the moments when I could fully throw myself into the present, some of this heaviness was temporarily lifted. During this time, Ginger regarded me with a kindness that felt like a silent appreciation of my presence. In turn, I lay on the carpet beside her and marveled at her fierce calmness. She seemed to be completely at peace with and fully aware of what was happening to her. It was almost as if she were patiently waiting for the angel of death to spirit her away.

These end-of-life experiences with Ginger come to mind as I watch my present cat companion edge into her senior years. My heart tightens at the thought of saying the last goodbye to my dear Tawy. To cushion the blow of this traumatic experience, I try to maintain a background awareness of her impermanence. But I also want to stay present, which I do by consciously appreciating her wonderful qualities.

When I focus on the Tawy now, I stroke her with increased awareness, relishing the downy softness of her coat. I pay more attention to the vibration of her purrs, her high-pitched meows, and the endearing way she lowers her eyelids to express deep contentment. When she flips over to expose her irresistibly fluffy belly, I happily bury my fingers in her thicket of wild tufts. Appreciating her like this feels like savoring dark chocolate with its slightly bitter edge. The enjoyment is tinged with the tart truth of Tawy's impermanence.

Cat Gratitude

Despite liking to hang out near me, Snappy was never the kind of cat who would lie in my lap. So after sixteen years together, I was quite shocked when she spontaneously hopped up on me one afternoon. I was even more astonished when she positioned herself to face me, purred loudly, and stared at me so ardently that I felt bathed in adoration. I was so captivated by her intense display of affection that I stroked her tiger-striped fur repeatedly to keep her motor humming. We spent about ten minutes locked in this warm, energetic embrace, until I just couldn't ignore my bladder's urgent call anymore.

About a week later, Snappy had a few episodes of coughing and vomiting. I thought the new medication was the culprit, so I stopped giving it to her. However, the very next day I found her tucked under the stairs and breathing heavily. Alarmed, I immediately toted her off to the vet.

My vet at that time was a gentle and personable man. He carefully assessed Snappy, while I waited anxiously for his verdict. In a kindly voice, he began, "Her lungs are filling up with fluid. We could subject her to a battery of tests to determine the cause. But even if we discover the problem, there is nothing we could do to save her. Unfortunately, she will have to be put to sleep. Would you still like us to perform the tests?"

An emotional tidal wave was rising inside and threatening to engulf me. Since I wanted to be fully present with Snappy until her last breath, I refused to get pulled into the strong current and have it take me away from being completely engaged. So I chose to focus my mind on the present.

This cleared my mind enough to opt for putting a speedy end to Snappy's suffering, rather than holding onto the false hope that the tests might provide us better options. I believed this was the best course of action, especially since Snappy was exuding an extraordinary aplomb that told me she knew the end was near. She seemed to be patiently awaiting her deliverance.

The vet left to prepare the medication. Replicating her behavior of a week ago, Snappy began to fix my gaze with fierce affection and vigorous purrs. Snappy's actions were so reminiscent of the prior week that I was certain she was trying to tell me something. And what she seemed to be conveying was her immense gratitude. I felt she was thanking me for consistently filling her belly with food and her heart with love. So in return, I laid a supportive hand on her heaving abdomen and used my voice and eyes to radiate love back to her.

The vet softly reentered the room. As soon as he administered the fatal serum, it took hold, erasing from her eyes all traces of the Snappy I knew. Her purring pulse petered out, followed by the slow stiffening and cooling of her flesh.

Deeply saddened, I returned home to hug my remaining feline companion and appreciate the willingness of my boyfriend to be with me in my grief.

In the aftermath of Snappy's death, I realized she left me with a lasting gift. The memory of her passionate displays of gratitude has helped me cope with all subsequent losses. With each fresh loss I've endured, I have been quick to feel gratitude for everything that newly departed being ever brought to my life. The sweetness of these blessings feels like a taste of honey amidst a bitter brew!

The Compassionate Cat

Our pets can be wonderful consolers in an emotional crisis. Their behavior in such times has taught me about compassion.

In one particularly striking incidence of cat compassion, I suddenly burst into tears while feeling intensely sad. From clear across the room, Snappy immediately bounded over to my side and plopped against me. Then she looked at me with wide, caring eyes, and transmitted her love and empathy through reassuring purrs. Just having her beside me was a soothing balm to my tearful soul. Her compassionate behavior helped me feel a little less alone in the world.

Reflecting on this incident, I realize how important it is to give and receive compassion. Though we generally cannot make another person's pain disappear, the very least we can do is express some care and empathy. I also know that the practice of developing compassion creates a reservoir of feelings that remain on tap, ready to be poured out when someone is suffering too greatly. By my caring words and actions I can convey, "There, there, my dear, here's a cup of compassion for you!"

Tending to a sick or dying cat has been a way for me to develop compassion. Karuna naturally springs up when I'm feeling badly for my suffering cat. I'm also spurred to action, willing to do just about anything to ease his or her pain.

When Ginger was approaching death, she was so weak that she was unable to move from a spot on the hallway carpet. It was nighttime, and I was ready to spend the night camped on the ground beside her. My compassion for her waning constitution was more important to me in those moments than the comfort and coziness of my bed. So I started to throw down some pillows and blankets to prepare the area for our remaining time together.

But in the middle of my ministrations, Ginger started to wail woefully. Actually, it was more of a horrifying croak that seemed to emanate from the depths of her being. I quickly realized she was in excruciating pain and that the most caring thing I could do for her would be to take her to the vet to put her out of her misery. I knew this journey could not wait until a more convenient time, such as the next morning. I gently placed her into her cardboard carrier and sped her to the emergency clinic, despite being physically and emotionally drained from a prolonged week of providing her hospice.

I worked at maintaining my composure as I heard Ginger's painful howls. I answered her cries in the most loving and calming tones I could muster, belying the fear and tremendous sadness that roiled inside me. With the top of the carrier open, I used my eyes to beam warm feelings into her wide, terror-struck orbs.

When I had brought Snappy to the vet to receive her fatal injection, a few years prior, she purred loudly, locking eyes with me. We exchanged our intense love for each other as she received that last, swift shot. After such a beautiful experience, I anticipated that Ginger's transition would be just as lovely. Yet, Ginger's suffering was far too great for her to be her usual cherubic self. Her uncharacteristic agitation at this time signaled to me that we would not have the same wonderful send-off. I belatedly realized that I would have to continue to offer Ginger as much love and compassion as possible without expecting it to be reciprocated. Instead, I had to openly and warmly receive her edginess.

We soon reached the vet. I lifted Ginger out of the car. She had always been a lightweight cat, but now the carrier felt practically weightless.

Fairly quickly after we entered the emergency ward, we were admitted into the procedure room. The vastness of this space, with its stainless steel surfaces, colorless walls, and large windows into the surrounding operating rooms, only accentuated my grief. Carefully, I lifted Ginger out of her carrier and laid her across the metal table. I slowly petted her until the doctor came and administered the injection.

With this medicinal act of compassion, my dear friend was instantly released from her suffering forever.

About the Author

Judy Taylor is a nonfiction author and poet. Her previous book, Living Lightly with Lyme, is available through Amazon and Smashwords. She has also published several essays and poetry in recent editions of Passing It On. Judy enjoys life in the San Francisco Bay Area writing, doing photography, and living simply.

www.ingramcontent.com/pod-product-compliance
Lightning Source LLC
Chambersburg PA
CBHW072112290426
44110CB00014B/1894